4/1/10

BY VALERIE BODDEN

CREATIVE EDUCATION

Published by Creative Education
P.O. Box 227, Mankato, Minnesota 56002
Creative Education is an imprint of The Creative Company
www.thecreativecompany.us

Design and production by The Design Lab
Art direction by Rita Marshall
Printed in the United States of America

Photographs by 123RF (Dmitry Rukhlenko), Big Stock Photo
(Bobby Singapore), Corbis (Corbis Sygma, Wolfgang Kaehler, Layne
Kennedy, Danny Lehman, Buddy Mays, Reuters, Galen Rowell,
Kevin Schafer, Sea World of California, Nik Wheeler, Staffan
Widstrand), Dreamstime (Sunheyy), iStockphoto (Emre Ogan)

Library of Congress Cataloging-in-Publication Data
Bodden, Valerie.
Amazon River / by Valerie Bodden.
p. cm. — (Big outdoors)
Summary: A fundamental introduction to the Amazon River,
including the rainforests that surround it, the creatures that live
in it, and how people have affected its tropical environment.
Includes index.
ISBN 978-1-58341-814-7
1. Amazon River—Juvenile literature. I. Title. II. Series.

F2546.B597 2010
981'.1—dc22   2009004590

First Edition
9 8 7 6 5 4 3 2 1

AMAZON RIVER

The Amazon River is the second-longest river in the world. It is on the **continent** of South America. The Amazon River flows through the countries of Peru, Colombia, and Brazil. It ends in the Atlantic Ocean.

SOUTH ★ AMERICA

The Amazon River takes many twists and turns through the land

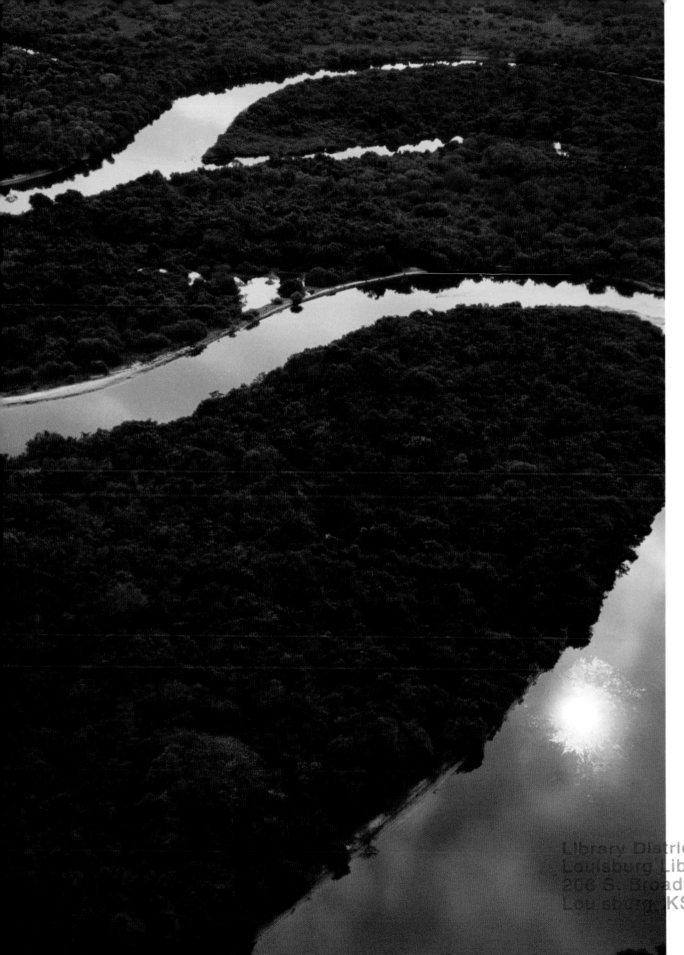

AMAZON RIVER

5

BIG OUTDOORS

People sometimes call the Amazon River the "Ocean River."

The Amazon River is about 4,000 miles (6,400 km) long. It holds more water than any other river in the world. The water in the Amazon River is muddy.

The Amazon is very wide in some parts but very narrow in others

Scientists think that the Amazon River used to flow west toward the Pacific Ocean. But then the Andes Mountains rose up. They blocked the river's path. So it began to flow east toward the Atlantic Ocean.

When the river has to flow over tall rocks, it makes a waterfall

The only waterfalls on the Amazon River are in the Andes Mountains.

The Amazon River floods every year, so homes nearby are built on **stilts.**

The weather around the Amazon River is warm year-round. It rains a lot there. There are a few big cities along the Amazon River. Some groups of **native** peoples live near the river, too.

Homes built on stilts (above) can stay dry during most floods

Much of the land around the Amazon River is covered by a huge rainforest. Trees grow close together in the rainforest. Monkeys, jaguars, and iguanas live in the rainforest. So do parrots and sloths.

Iguanas (above) and parrots (opposite) are colorful animals

About half of all the kinds of birds in the world live near the Amazon River.

The Amazon River's pirarucu (*pih-RAH-rih-koo*) is one of the world's biggest freshwater fish.

Fish such as piranhas (*pih-RAH-nuhs*) swim in the Amazon River. So do animals such as pink river dolphins and **manatees**. Snakes live in the water, too. Giant Amazon water lilies float on the river.

About 20 kinds of piranhas (above) live in the Amazon River

Native peoples have lived near the Amazon River for a long time. The first white people arrived at the Amazon River about 500 years ago. They studied the river and the rainforest.

Many native people still travel on the river in wooden canoes

Over the years, people have cut down many trees near the Amazon River. They have **polluted** the water. They have built **dams** on the rivers that join the Amazon. But today, people work to protect the Amazon River.

Large trees are cut down and made into wooden boards for houses

Many people visit the Amazon River every year. They take boat rides down the river. They fish in the water. And they are amazed by all the plants and animals in the Amazon rainforest!

Some visitors ride down the Amazon River on big cruise ships

Some plants from the Amazon rainforest are used to make headache medicines.

Glossary

continent one of Earth's seven big pieces of land

dams walls built across rivers to hold water back

manatees big water animals with paddle-shaped front flippers and a flat tail

native original; native peoples were the first to live in an area

polluted made dirty with chemicals or other things that are bad for the earth, water, or air

stilts tall posts that hold a building off the ground

Read More about It

Darling, Kathy. *Amazon ABC*. New York: Lothrop, Lee & Shepard Books, 1996.

Schulte, Mary. *The Amazon River*. New York: Children's Press, 2006.

Index

Andes Mountains 8, 9
animals 12, 13, 14,
    15, 20
Atlantic Ocean 4, 8
dams 19
natives 11, 16
plants 12, 15, 19,
    20, 22

pollution 19
rainforests 12, 16,
    20, 22
size 4, 7
South America 4
visitors 19
weather 11